Book Projects to Send Home

Grade 5

Published by Instructional Fair
an imprint of Carson-Dellosa Publishing

Authors: Lori Sanders & Linda Kimble
Editor: Rebecca Warren

Instructional Fair
An imprint of Carson-Dellosa Publishing LLC
P.O. Box 35665
Greensboro, NC 27425 USA

© 2004 Carson-Dellosa Publishing LLC. The purchase of this material entitles the buyer to reproduce worksheets and activities for classroom use only—not for commercial resale. Reproduction of these materials for an entire school or district is prohibited. No part of this book may be reproduced (except as noted above), stored in a retrieval system, or transmitted in any form or by any means (mechanically, electronically, recording, etc.) without the prior written consent of Carson-Dellosa Publishing LLC. Instructional Fair is an imprint of Carson-Dellosa Publishing LLC.

Printed in Minster, OH USA • All rights reserved.   ISBN 978-0-7424-2735-8

2 3 4 5 6 7 8 9 10 GLO 15 14 13 12 11 10   244107784

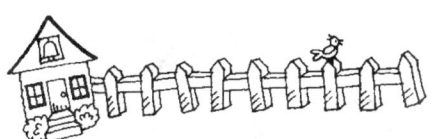 # Table of Contents

Introduction 4
Letter to Send Home 5
Genres of Literature 6

Book Project Activities

Clue Crew Board Game
Teacher Guide 7
Student Pages 8–10

Fiction Friend
Teacher Guide 11
Student Pages 12–14

Editorial Bumper Sticker
Teacher Guide 15
Student Pages 16–18

Flip-It Fact Book
Teacher Guide 19
Student Pages 20–22

It's in the News
Teacher Guide 23
Student Pages 24–26

Lit Kit
Teacher Guide 27
Student Pages 28–30

Role-Play
Teacher Guide 31
Student Pages 32–34

Mystery Marionette
Teacher Guide 35
Student Pages 36–38

Quality Character Banner
Teacher Guide 39
Student Pages 40–42

Far-Out Travel Brochure
Teacher Guide 43
Student Pages 44–46

Student Self-Evaluation Form 47
Suggested Titles for Fifth-Grade Readers 48

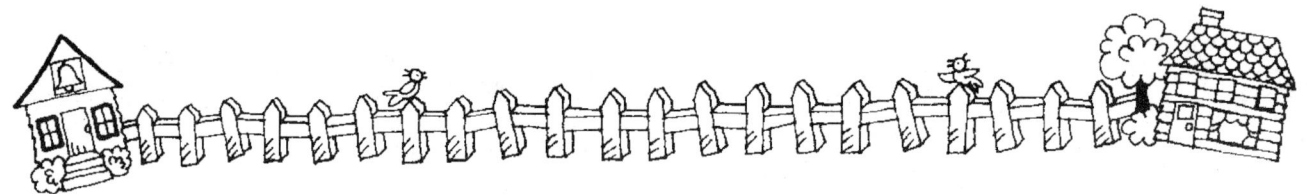

Introduction

School-to-home book projects are a wonderful means of encouraging enthusiasm for reading. In *Book Projects to Send Home*, you will find ten creative projects to encourage students to read outside of school and then demonstrate their comprehension in enjoyable ways.

Here is a blueprint for using this book's resources:

1. You may use the letter on page 5 to introduce families to the program or to send home with each project. Students bring back the cut-off slip at the bottom of the page showing that someone at home understands the project and knows the due date.

2. Each book project includes instructions that explain the project in detail, give a list of materials, provide step-by-step assembly information, and detail the manner in which work will be shared in class.

3. You may use the genres of literature explanations on page 6 to aid in student book selection.

4. Each set of student instructions is followed by an activity sheet that can be used in class or sent home with students. The activity sheet provides brainstorming ideas to help students begin thinking about the project.

5. The form on page 47 provides a way for students to assess their own work on projects.

Incorporating this easy-to-implement home/school connection will be a worthwhile complement to your classroom reading instruction. You will be thrilled with the way your students demonstrate creativity and understanding through their work.

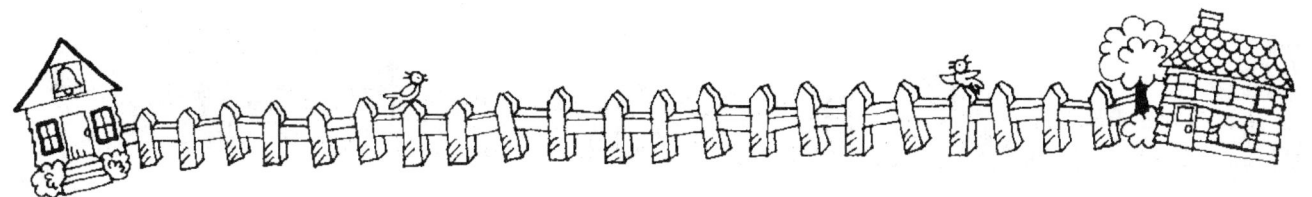

Dear Friends,

Your child will be asked to read a book and then demonstrate his/her comprehension through creative projects completed at home. These projects will encourage thinking skills and will give your child a chance to develop other skills as well, such as responsibility, initiative, effort, and problem solving.

I will offer guidance regarding book selection, and I must approve your child's book selection for each project. Books may come from your home or from our library.

Please sign and return the form at the bottom of the page. This will allow me to keep a record that each student received and understood the project requirements. Encourage your child to be responsible for keeping his/her own schedule for completing the project.

I look forward to seeing your child's reading skills grow and am confident that these projects will help to foster that growth.

Sincerely,

Please Sign and Return

_____'s family has received the book project instructions for the _____ project.

We are aware that the project is due on _____.

Signature _____

Student Signature _____

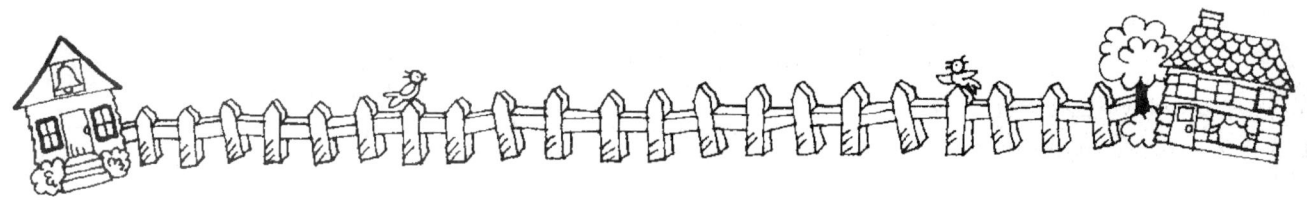

Genres of Literature

autobiography—the story of a real person's life that is written in the person's own words

biography—the story of a real person's life that is written by someone other than that person

fiction—a story about a made-up person or place; **realistic fiction** is about a person or an event that could happen in today's world (*see also* **historical fiction** and **science fiction**)

folktale—a tale that has been told out loud for generations; includes certain predictable phrases and character types

fairy tale—a type of folktale that includes stories about fairies or other made-up people or places

historical fiction—a story about a made-up person during a realistic period of history; includes details about the historical setting

nonfiction—a book filled with information and facts on a specific topic; is about things in the real world

poetry—a type of writing that uses language in special ways, such as rhyme and rhythm, to create pictures and feelings in the reader's mind

science fiction—a story about a made-up place that often happens in the future; includes new gadgets and inventions that do not exist in the world today

Clue Crew Board Game

Teacher Guide

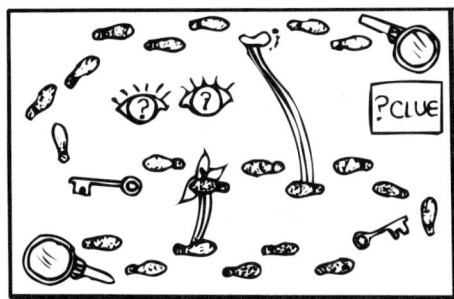

Skills Covered

- identifying the setting
- sequence of events
- using the writing process

Project Description

Students design and construct a board game that illustrates and depicts the setting and sequence of events from selected mystery novels. Students have the opportunity to play other students' games and learn about other selections in the genre.

Material Suggestions

You may want to provide students with precut poster board to keep the size of the final projects the same.

Tips to Introduce

Displaying commercial board games may help students generate ideas about appropriate and creative designs. You could conduct a brainstorm session to list ideas.

Classroom Connections

What makes a good mystery? Ask students if they have ever read a mystery that they solved before the end of the book, and have them explain how they did it. To get students thinking about the elements of mystery stories, rent a mystery to show to the class, stopping it at various points to see if students noticed clues or plot twists. Public television has offered hour-long productions of many famous mystery stories by authors such as Sir Arthur Conan Doyle, Agatha Christie, Josephine Tey, and others. Many of these are available on video or DVD.

Display and Presentation

Games can be kept available for students to use at a reading center throughout the month. Divide the students into small groups and have them alternate the games so that they can study the rules of each game before playing, either alone or with partners.

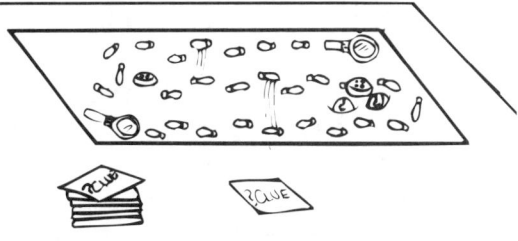

Clue Crew Board Game

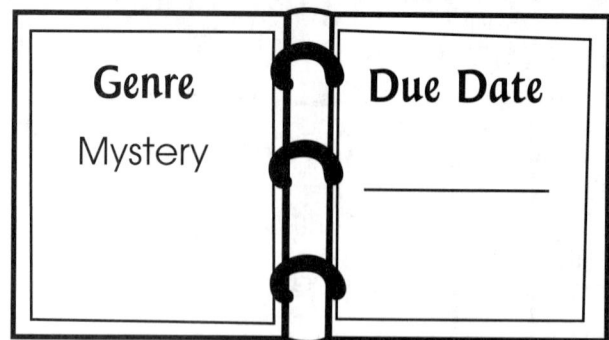

Genre Mystery

Due Date _____

After choosing and reading an exciting mystery book, your task is to design a Clue Crew game board that depicts the setting and provides the sequence of main events of your selection. Classmates who play the game should learn what happened in the book you read.

Material Suggestions

Poster board, a pair of dice, index cards, markers or colored pencils, objects for game pieces (use buttons, beads, decorated bottle caps, checkers).

Project Requirements

1. Select a mystery and have it approved. Start reading. As you read, list key events that lead to the solution of the mystery. Use the form on page 10 to help you record events as you read.

2. Collect materials to construct your game board. Sketch your game board on paper first, and check against your book for accuracy. Revise and edit your sketch with an adult. Decide what picture or image you want to use for the background.

3. Produce the completed game board, adding color and detail. Be sure to include challenges, such as "lose a turn" squares. Have squares where instruction cards are drawn, too.

4. Cut apart index cards to make 10 to 15 small game cards for player instructions, such as "Joe got sick and missed school. Lose one turn." "Joe finds a footprint clue. Take an extra turn." Use plot twists and details that the character really experienced in the book you read.

Clue Crew Board Game

5. Make or find game pieces that relate to the book you read. For example, use small cars for a mystery about auto racing. Or decorate place markers made of buttons with stickers or pictures that relate to the book.

6. Complete and cut out the Project Designer's Tag. Glue or tape it to the back of your game board. Put your game pieces in a small bag or container.

7. Write detailed instructions for how to play your game, and mount them on a separate piece of poster board.

Here is your schedule for the Clue Crew Board Game project:

- ☐ Week 1—Select mystery. Have it approved. Read.
- ☐ Week 2—Read. List key events. Sketch game board.
- ☐ Week 3—Design game board. Make cards and other game pieces.
- ☐ Week 4—Draft rules. Edit, rewrite, mount on poster board.

Check When Done

Presentation Guidelines

Your game will teach your classmates about the great mystery you enjoyed. We will be playing your game in class.

Clue Crew Board Game

Brainstorm

Use the form below to help you think about the events of your mystery story.

First, this happens: _____

Then, this happens: _____

Then, this happens: _____

When this happens, it's obvious how the mystery will be solved: _____
_____

At the end of the story, _____
_____.

Before You Turn It In

1. Does the game board convey the correct sequence in the story?
2. Are your instructions clear enough to allow classmates to understand and play the game?

Project Designer's Tag

Clue Crew Board Game Project
Name _____
Title of Book _____
Author _____
Genre _____
Date _____

Fiction Friend

Teacher Guide

Skills Covered
- identifying character traits
- conducting an interview
- using the writing process

Project Description
Students design life-sized book characters that are dressed appropriately for the time period of their books and display the personality of the character. Each student creates a question-and-answer interview script to demonstrate understanding of the character. Completed interviews hang around the characters' necks and serve as introductions.

Material Suggestions
Students need to provide their own materials for costumes. You may take part by offering a class "rag bag" with items found in a local thrift shop.

Tips to Introduce
If you choose not to model the construction of a book character, you may receive a broader range of creative solutions and original designs. Make a decision for your individual class, based on their art abilities. Either way, plan on modeling the creation of an interview. Use a classroom read-aloud selection. Pretend you are the main character and have students ask you questions.

Classroom Connections
A comparison of clothing from different periods of history gives you a great social studies tie-in to this book project. Find some interesting comparisons in costume source books or in period paintings. Ask students why styles might change; reasons vary from economics, to religious beliefs, to how a monarch's personal tastes affected styles at court. Talk about clothing differences between various social classes and for different kinds of work. Help students to realize how fashion is tied to many other social issues. During a free-writing period, ask students to write about current fashions. Ask: What's in style now? How do you feel about current clothing styles? Is there clothing from another time period that you might have liked better?

Display and Presentation
These life-sized characters make a great impression when hung in a hallway or in the lobby of a school. You may choose to celebrate this project by inviting guests to the classroom to "meet" the characters as each one is introduced by the designer.

Fiction Friend

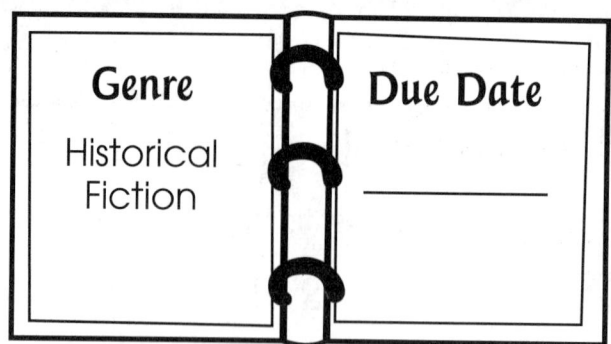

Choose a character from a historical fiction book and turn him or her into a three-dimensional, life-sized character! You will also create interview questions and answers. This will help you introduce your character to our class.

Material Suggestions

Corrugated cardboard, poster board, old clothing, head gear and foot gear (borrow cast-off Halloween costumes, check the rag basket, or visit a local thrift shop). You may also want to use markers, yarn or string for hair, and paints to add facial details.

Project Requirements

1. Select a historical fiction book and have it approved. Read the book carefully. Choose a character you like. As you read, make notes about the character's clothing, likes and dislikes, home and family.

2. Create your life-sized character. You may choose to stuff clothing to make a three-dimensional character. Or, you can tape together sections of poster board or cardboard to make a flat life-sized figure. The choice is yours.

3. Dress your character in appropriate clothing for the time period. Use actual clothing or wallpaper, wrapping paper, and/or fabric scraps. Design the character's face and expression.

4. Create a way to display your character. You may want to make a stand, use a wire hanger to create a hook, or make a hanging loop from twine or utility cord.

Fiction Friend

5. Next, compose interview questions. Answer each question from the viewpoint of your character. See page 14 for ideas.

6. Revise and edit the draft of your interview. Then write or type a clean copy.

7. Mount the final version of the interview on cardboard. Punch two holes at the top and string yarn through the holes. Hang this around the neck of the character to finish your display.

8. Complete and cut out the Project Designer's Tag. Tape it to the back of the interview "necklace."

Here is your schedule for the Fiction Friend project:

☐ Week 1—Choose book. Get approval. Read.

☐ Week 2—Choose character. Make notes. Collect materials.

☐ Week 3—Design and make character.

☐ Week 4—Draft and edit interview. Make interview "necklace" for character.

Check When Done

Presentation Guidelines

You may be asked to read one or more of your interview questions and answers to the class. The interview should help audience members to understand your character, even if they haven't read the book. This project might attract attention when you're transporting it to school. Just smile and wave!

© Carson-Dellosa   0-7424-2735-8 *Book Projects to Send Home*

Fiction Friend

Brainstorm
Answer the questions as if you were the main character.
1. What problem did you have and how did you solve it?
   _____

2. Who is the most important person in your life? Why?
   _____

3. What is your home like?
   _____

4. What do you hope to do in the future?
   _____

Before You Turn It In
1. Is your life-sized character well designed, detailed, and dressed in period costume?
2. Is your interview script clear, descriptive, and does it show knowledge of character?

Project Designer's Tag

Fiction Friend Project
Name _____
Title of Book _____
Author _____
Genre _____
Date _____

© Carson-Dellosa | 0-7424-2735-8 *Book Projects to Send Home*

Editorial Bumper Sticker

Teacher Guide

Skills Covered
- persuasive writing
- supporting an opinion
- using the writing process

Project Description
Students read about an environmental topic such as rain forests, an endangered species, or air pollution. After forming an opinion about a topic, each student writes a convincing letter to the editor. Students also create bumper stickers that alert people to the importance of their chosen topics.

Material Suggestions
Writing paper, colored paper for the bumper stickers, markers or paints.

Tips to Introduce
Bring a newspaper editorial page to class and read appropriate letters to the editor out loud. Note the various ways that the writers back up their opinions. Then discuss the components of a strong letter. Show students how research will help them formulate opinions based on the facts they find.

Classroom Connections
Ask students to look for examples of bumper stickers, buttons, or campaign posters. If you can find samples of these materials from the past, you can talk about the similarities and differences to today's style. You can also compare social and environmental issues from different eras in history.

Display and Presentation
Create or have students make large paper car cutouts. Bumper stickers can be placed randomly on these cars as part of a hallway display. Use the headline "You Auto Pay Attention to Important Issues."

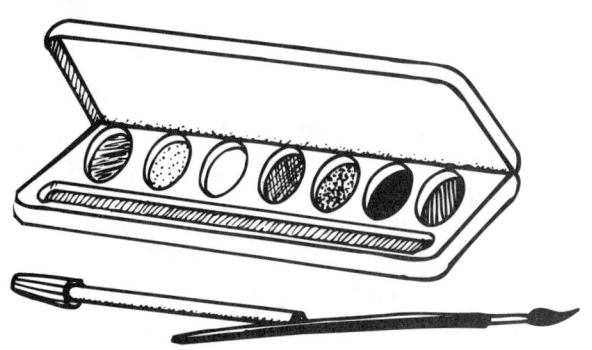

© Carson-Dellosa · 15 · 0-7424-2735-8 *Book Projects to Send Home*

Editorial Bumper Sticker

Genre
One nonfiction book, six newspaper articles, or three magazine articles

Due Date
_____

After reading about an environmental topic such as rain forests, an endangered species, or air pollution, you will form your own opinion on the topic. Then, you will write a convincing letter to the editor to persuade people of your view. You will also create a bumper sticker to remind our class of the importance of your topic.

Material Suggestions

Writing paper for letter, colored or glossy paper (4" x 11") for bumper sticker, markers or acrylic paint pens.

Project Requirements

1. Select your reading material on an environmental topic of interest. Have your topic approved.

2. Read selection(s) and take notes. Pay special attention to both sides of any issue related to your topic. Use the form on page 18 to take notes.

3. Create a rough-draft letter to the editor of an imaginary newspaper, expressing your own opinion on the issue. Add power to your viewpoint by stating facts you discovered in the reading material.

4. Ask an adult at home to read your letter and offer comments or ask for clarification. Revise and edit your letter.

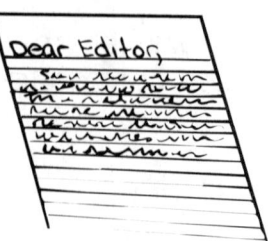

5. Create a clean copy of the letter and add your signature.

Editorial Bumper Sticker

6. Next, brainstorm "catchy" phrases for your bumper sticker about the environmental topic you chose.

7. Design a rough draft of a bumper sticker on a 4" x 11" rectangle of scratch paper. Use the best phrase that you wrote. Sketch in your bumper sticker phrase, artwork, background, and borders.

8. Transfer the bumper sticker slogan to your paper of choice.

9. Fill the background with detail, adding color with markers or paints.

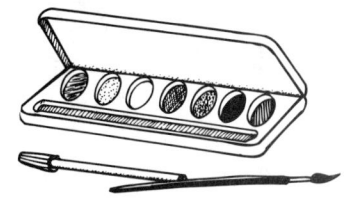

Here is your schedule for the Editorial Bumper Sticker project:

☐ Week 1—Choose topic. Read resource materials (book, magazine articles, or newspaper articles).

☐ Week 2—Finish reading. Draft letter to editor. Have adult read. Edit.

☐ Week 3—Write slogan. Design and complete your bumper sticker.

Check When Done

Presentation Guidelines

You will read your letter to classmates, who will have an opportunity to agree or disagree with the stated main point before your writing is shared. After hearing your letter read, classmates will again vote, with the opportunity to change their opinions. We may do this by secret ballot or a show of hands.

Editorial Bumper Sticker

Brainstorm

Issue: _____

What some people think about this issue: _____
_____
    Fact _____
    Fact _____

What other people think about this issue: _____
_____
    Fact _____
    Fact _____

What I think about this issue: _____
_____
    Reason _____
    Reason _____

Before You Turn It In

1. Is your letter to the editor persuasive, strongly written, and full of facts to back up your opinion?
2. Does your bumper sticker have a strong or funny slogan and an eye-catching design?

Project Designer's Tag

Editorial Bumper Sticker Project
Name _____
Title of Book _____
Author _____
Genre _____
Date _____

Flip-It Fact Book

Teacher Guide

Skills Covered

- reading nonfiction books
- note-taking
- organizing information

Project Description

Students create a Flip-It Fact Book after reading a nonfiction selection. The student first creates a one-paragraph proposal, stating why the book was chosen. Then the student lists questions that indicate what he/she wants to learn from the information in the book. After brainstorming a total of 15 to 20 questions, students choose the 10 best to put into a flip book. Questions are written on one side of a page and answers (when discovered in the book) are written on the flip side.

Material Suggestions

You may supply 10 half-sheets of paper (8 1/2" x 11" paper cut in half width-wise), front and back cover paper, and brad clips or book rings. If you have students supply their own paper, you may still want to make brad clips available.

Tips to Introduce

Create a class Flip-It Fact Book with information learned from a theme study. Come up with a list of questions as a class that students hope to learn from a new unit. Once the unit is finished, return to the list and see if students can fill in the answers. After creating this format in a group setting, students should have guidelines to succeed with this project at home.

Classroom Connections

Tie into this book project with some class time devoted to the concept of questions. Make students aware of different kinds of questions. In addition to a study of the five Ws, students will benefit from a refined understanding of the purpose behind questions. For example, a question to get information about a fact ("What time is dinner?") is the same sentence form, but different in intent from a question that elicits an opinion ("What is your favorite thing to eat for dinner?").

Display and Presentation

Have students share project questions from "the author's chair" to see if classmates know the answers. Misconceptions should be acknowledged, but not corrected. Instead, students should be encouraged to read a certain page in the book to gain knowledge about the topic on their own.

© Carson-Dellosa   19   0-7424-2735-8 Book Projects to Send Home

Flip-It Fact Book

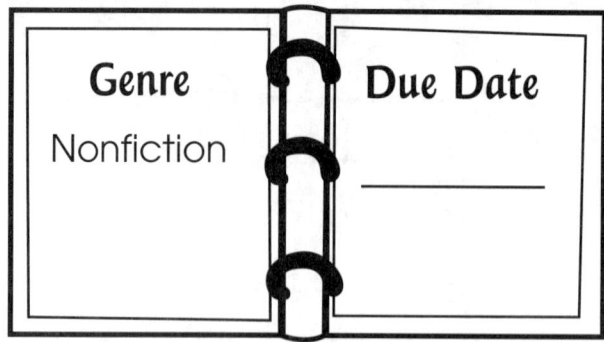

After choosing a nonfiction book for this project, you will write a one-paragraph statement about what you hope to learn from the book. Use the chart on page 22 to help you record your questions before and after reading. Then you'll make a Flip-It Fact Book and record answers as you read. Make your questions interesting enough so others will want to learn more about the topic you chose!

Material Suggestions

You will need 10 half-sheets of paper, construction paper for book covers, your brad clips or book rings from class, and pencils, pens, markers, and/or colored pencils.

Project Requirements

1. Select a book. Write a paragraph stating what you hope to learn from your reading. Have the paragraph approved.

2. Before you read your book, draft a list of 15 to 20 possible questions you may have about the topic.

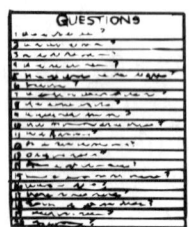

3. Review your 15 to 20 draft questions and select the 10 best. Have an adult help you to revise and edit them.

4. Cut five sheets of $8\frac{1}{2}$" x 11" paper widthwise so each sheet is $8\frac{1}{2}$" x $5\frac{1}{2}$". Punch two to three holes along the top of all the pages. Use construction paper to make covers and punch them as well. Insert brads or book rings to make your flip book.

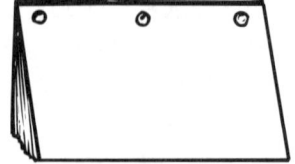

5. On the front of each page, record a question you've selected.

© Carson-Dellosa   20   0-7424-2735-8 Book Projects to Send Home

Flip-It Fact Book

6. Now read your book. As you find the answer to each question, write it on the flip side of the page.

7. Add some illustrations, borders, and creative lettering to offer visual interest. Decorate the front cover.

8. Complete and cut out the Project Designer's Tag and glue to the back cover.

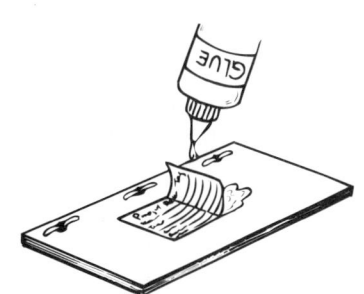

Here is your schedule for the Flip-It Fact Book project:

☐ Week 1—Draft paragraph about chosen book. Have it approved. Draft questions.

☐ Week 2—Choose questions. Rewrite questions and make book.

☐ Week 3—Read and record answers.

☐ Week 4—Finish reading. Decorate book.

Check When Done

Presentation Guidelines

You will have the opportunity to share your book from "the author's chair" by reading your questions to the class. See if your classmates already know the answers or have misconceptions about your topic. Refer listeners to your Flip-It Fact Book for the right information.

Flip-It Fact Book

Brainstorm

Use the form below to help you organize your questions before reading and the answers you've discovered after reading.

Before Reading— What I Want to Know	After Reading— What I Learned

Before You Turn It In

1. Are your questions challenging and interesting?
2. Do your answers show comprehension of material and are they clearly presented?

Project Designer's Tag

Flip-It Fact Book Project
Name _____
Title of Book _____
Author _____
Genre _____
Date _____

© Carson-Dellosa

It's in the News

Teacher Guide

Skills Covered
- reading a biography
- summarizing
- using the writing process
- organizing information for oral presentations

Project Description
Students act as reporters for an imaginary newspaper. After reading the biography of a famous person, each student writes either a personal profile article or a feature story about an important event in the life of the person. Each student entices others to read his or her article by presenting a one-minute "newscast" that summarizes the person's life or the selected event.

Material Suggestions
Students will require only writing materials for this project. You may wish to look for a hand-held microphone to add flair to the "newscast" presentations.

Tips to Introduce
To inspire enthusiasm for this project, role-play real-life careers in the news world, such as a reporter or newscaster. Include brainstorming, note-taking, research, and interviewing skills as part of the role-play. Show a videotape of a typical local or national newscast, and follow with a discussion of project expectations.

Classroom Connections
A classroom discussion or unit about the concept of fame might add an interesting dimension to this book project. Talk about various accomplishments that make people famous, and how much they can differ: discovering the cure for a disease, hitting a home run, acting in a television show, creating a fast-food chain of restaurants. Follow up with a free-writing exercise where students pretend that they have done something that has made them famous. Ask each student to describe an accomplishment and state how fame has changed his or her life.

Display and Presentation
Compile the project articles into a class news booklet to display in the school or classroom library. Individual articles could also be mounted on classroom or hallway bulletin boards. Have students make one-minute newscasts highlighting the most interesting points in their article to the class.

It's in the News

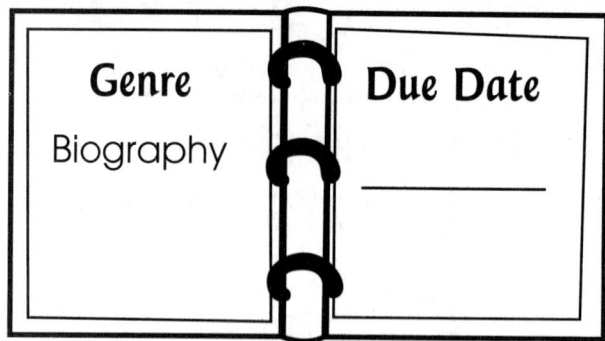

You are a reporter for a world-famous newspaper! You have been assigned to write an article about a famous national or world figure after reading that person's biography. Decide whether to write about an important event in that person's life or compose a personal profile. Then, you will create a one-minute broadcast script from your article.

Material Suggestions

You will need paper and pencil or access to a computer and printer.

Project Requirements

1. Make your selection of a biography and have it approved. Begin reading. Use the time line on page 26 to record major events in the life of this person as you read.

2. Choose your article format from either of the options below.

   a. **Important Event Article**

   Write a feature story that covers the five Ws.
   - Who is the article about?
   - What did the individual do that was noteworthy?
   - When and where did the important event occur?
   - Why did the individual participate in this event? Include your views about how this person made a difference.

   b. **Personal Profile Article**

   Prepare a written description of the famous person.
   - Include significant personal facts, such as the person's age, details about his/her family, likes and dislikes.
   - To give an idea of how this person was viewed by others, discuss the opinions of people who knew him/her.
   - Give an overview of the person's life, featuring major accomplishments.

It's in the News

3. In either type of article, be sure to show why this person is important to history. Create an interesting headline that draws the reader's attention to your article.

4. For either article, create a rough draft to be edited and revised with an adult.

5. Write or type a clean copy of your newspaper article. Make a hand-drawn illustration of the event or person. Include a written caption beneath the picture.

6. Complete and cut out the Project Designer's Tag, and clip it to your article.

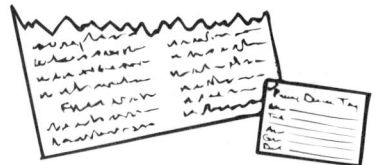

7. Prepare a one-minute newscast, featuring the most interesting points from your article. Have a family member time you as you rehearse.

Here is your schedule for the It's in the News project:

☐ Week 1—Choose book. Have it approved. Start reading.

☐ Week 2—Select article format and have it approved. Research facts. Write rough draft.

☐ Week 3—Revise article. Make a clean copy. Make illustrations and captions.

☐ Week 4—Prepare and rehearse newscast.

Check When Done

Presentation Guidelines

Our class will compile these articles with a cover page that names our newspaper. This news booklet will be displayed in our school or classroom library. You will be giving a newscast to our class. Your one-minute "blip" should hook your listeners into wanting to read your complete article. Tell just enough to interest and entice!

It's in the News

Brainstorm
Use the time line below to help you keep track of key events in the life of your famous person.

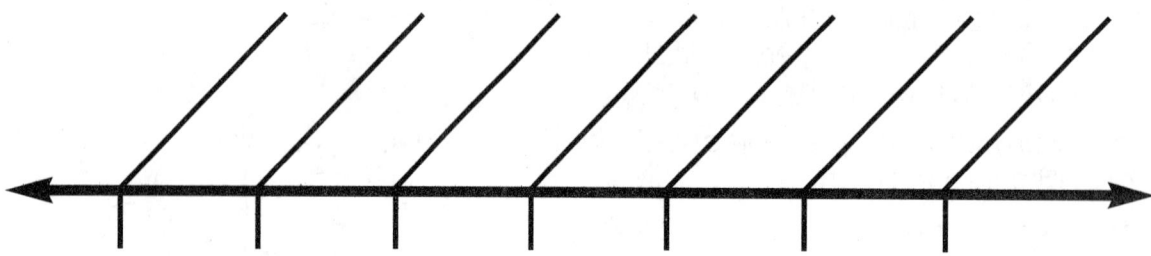

Most important event: _____

How this event changed history: _____
_____

Before You Turn It In
1. Does your article content show an understanding of the historical event or personality described?
2. Does your one-minute newscast offer enticing information about the person selected?

Project Designer's Tag

It's in the News Project
Name _____
Title of Book _____
Author _____
Genre _____
Date _____

© Carson-Dellosa

26

0-7424-2735-8 *Book Projects to Send Home*

Lit Kit

Teacher Guide

Skills Covered
- identifying story elements
- summarizing
- using the writing process

Project Description

Students create a poster board backdrop showing story elements (characters, setting, events, problem, and solution) from a novel they choose to read. Each element is labeled. The second part of this project involves creating a container related in shape or design to the book. This container holds five small props, either collected or created by the student. The props are used to retell the story to classmates.

Material Suggestions

Students provide their own art supplies for this project.

Tips to Introduce

It is important that students understand that the collection of props and the related containers will be used to help them retell the stories and engage the audience at the same time. Fifth graders are usually quite familiar with determining story elements of a novel, but it might be helpful to some if this were modeled with a read-aloud selection.

Classroom Connections

Our possessions show something about our personalities and about our personal "stories." Ask students to think about things they own, have collected, or have kept as mementoes. What makes an object meaningful? Ask them to imagine a "desert island" scenario. If they were stranded on a desert island, what three things would they want to have with them? (Exclude items for survival.) Ask them to list the objects and describe the reason why each one was chosen. You might wish to follow up with a session when each student chooses the most meaningful of the three objects and brings it into class.

Display and Presentation

The entire project can be displayed on students' desks or tables as part of a literature fair. The fair should involve invited guests, either from other classes or from the community. Guests will have the opportunity to comment on the projects and ask the students questions about their Lit Kits.

Lit Kit

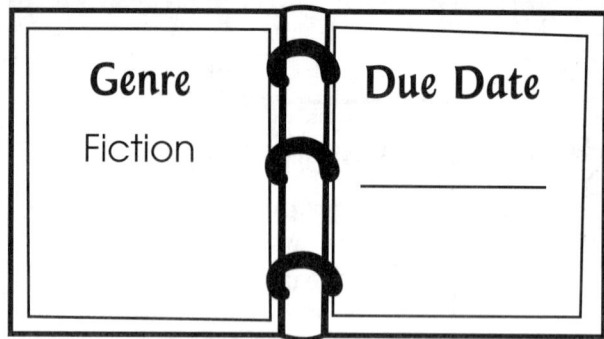

Genre Fiction

Due Date _____

This month, you will present a favorite book at our literature fair! You'll use a Lit Kit and backdrop to show the structure of the story you read. Entice others to read your book, based on your retelling and your choice of fascinating props.

Material Suggestions

The materials and props you need will vary, depending on your design and whether you need to make some of your props or not. You will need a container such as a cardboard box or other canister to house your Lit Kit.

Project Requirements

1. Choose a novel that you think you will love. Have it approved, and read it for pure enjoyment!

2. After reading, skim or reread the book a second time, making a list of possible props that you can make or collect to help you retell the story. Make notes about the characters, setting, important scenes, and the problem and solution of the story.

3. Find a shoebox, a wide-mouthed canister, or a similar-sized container big enough to hold your five props. Decorate the container to complement your book.

    For example: Create a ship, a log cabin, an old-fashioned trunk, a castle, a carousel, or a covered wagon.

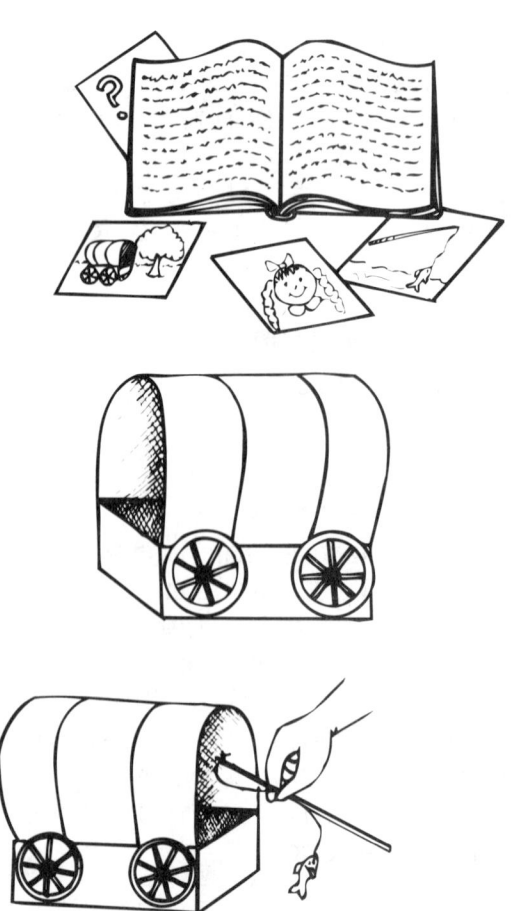

© Carson-Dellosa   28   0-7424-2735-8 *Book Projects to Send Home*

Lit Kit

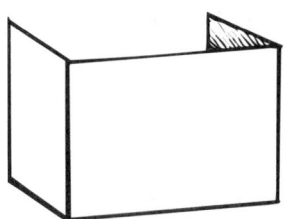

4. Now find or make the five props you have chosen from the book. These go inside your Lit Kit container.

5. Next, create your Lit Kit backdrop. Make a standing poster, at least 20" x 28". Each side will be folded in 6" to create a free-standing backdrop.

6. On this backdrop, you will write the title of the book, the name of the author, and the name of the illustrator. Then follow the steps below.

   a. Draw pictures to show important scenes. Draw and label each character, the setting, the problem, and the solution of the book. Use the chart on page 30 to take notes before you make your final copy. Make labels for these story elements. Each element should be drawn and labeled on a separate piece of paper and then mounted onto the backdrop. Be creative with lettering and paper shape.

   b. Remember to attach your completed Project Designer's Tag to the back of your Lit Kit.

Here is your schedule for the Lit Kit project:

☐ Week 1—Choose a work of fiction. Have it approved. Begin reading.

☐ Week 2—Read. List story elements and possible props. Choose a container.

☐ Week 3—Decorate container. Select and collect or make props. Complete Lit Kit.

☐ Week 4—Make and mount pictures and labels to create backdrop.

Check When Done

Presentation Guidelines

You will use the Lit Kit and backdrop to tell the story you chose to our class, highlighting main events. We'll invite guests to our literature fair so they can hear the stories and enjoy our displays.

Lit Kit

Brainstorm

Use the chart below to help you identify details about the story you read.

Characters	Setting	Problem	Main Events	Solution

Before You Turn It In

1. Is your Lit Kit container well designed and interesting to look at, and does it complement the book you chose?
2. Does your backdrop show scenes, setting, and characters from the story?

Project Designer's Tag

Lit Kit Project

Name _____

Title of Book _____

Author _____

Genre _____

Date _____

Role-Play

Teacher Guide

Skills Covered

- reading books set in other cultures
- identifying character traits
- summarizing a scene
- using the writing process

Project Description

Students read books set in another culture and choose a scene to act out for the class. Each student explains the scene by taking the role of a character and explaining the event in the first person. The student also is asked to create an appropriate artifact (prop) to aid in the telling of his or her story.

Material Suggestions

Encourage students to be innovative and original as they create their artifacts. Items could be painted, covered with fabric, or made to look old and weathered. Offer a few art tips or have students work on various techniques in art class.

Tips to Introduce

It is helpful to show a few examples of artifacts, so students understand the term. Read a picture book set in another culture aloud and ask the students to help you choose a scene that would be powerful to act out in first person. Create a short script together for the scene. Then determine an appropriate prop for the character to display or use. Discuss ways to create that artifact.

Classroom Connection

Compile a list of all the countries represented by your students' projects. Have a session where students locate these countries on a world map. You might want to use pushpins and a bulletin board to mark the locations. Break students into small groups and have them choose countries that interest them most. Then have each group complete a short research project to find general information about the country: its capital, its climate, its main exports, and what it might be like to live there. Each group should elect a spokesperson to present this information to the rest of the class.

Display and Presentation

Students will present their project retellings to the class or to other invited guests while using their handmade "artifact" props. After presentations, you can involve students in the creation of a class museum. Artifacts can be exhibited in a display titled "Art from Around the World."

Role-Play

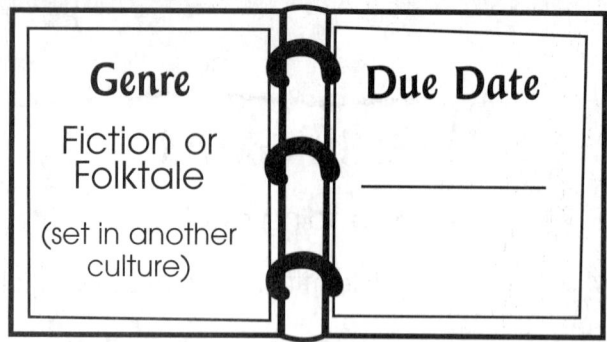

Genre
Fiction or Folktale
(set in another culture)

Due Date
_____

After reading a story set in another culture, you will choose a character and prepare to act that character's part in a significant scene. To make your character more authentic, you will create and decorate an "artifact"—a prop that this character used in the scene you have selected. After your presentation, your artifact will be displayed in a class museum.

Material Suggestions

The materials you choose will be unique to the prop you create. They could include papier mâché, a tin can, pressed leaves, or stones. You may need modeling clay or basket materials. Use your imagination and try to make your prop look like an authentic artifact from the story.

Project Requirements

1. Choose a book set in another culture. Have it approved. Begin reading.

2. After reading the book, choose an important scene and write or type the scene in the first person. Use the questions on page 34 to help you take notes about the scene. Make your scene sound as if you are the character, speaking from the "I" perspective. Explain the significance of your actions in the story. For example, in the fairy tale *Goldilocks and the Three Bears*, Goldilocks might say, "I'm Goldilocks. Yesterday I went to a cottage in the woods and saw . . ."

3. Edit your script and practice it in front of family members. It should take five minutes or less to act out your finished scene.

Role-Play

4. Next, choose a prop that is central to the scene. For example, Goldilocks might choose a porridge bowl. You could make a storybook-style bowl by layering papier mâché over a real cereal bowl. After it is dry, paint it a bright color with a patterned design. Remember that you must use your "artifact" in some way during your retelling.

5. Write a rough draft of a descriptive paragraph about your artifact. Be sure to include who used it and why it is important to the story. Revise, edit, and prepare a clean copy to be displayed with the artifact in our classroom museum.

6. Complete and cut out the Project Designer's Tag and attach it to your paragraph.

Here is your schedule for the Role-Play project:

- ☐ Week 1—Choose book. Have it approved. Start reading.
- ☐ Week 2—Select character and scene. Write script for scene. Edit and rehearse.
- ☐ Week 3—Choose artifact. Create.
- ☐ Week 4—Finish artifact. Compose and edit paragraph.

Check When Done

Presentation Guidelines

Remember that your scene needs to be in first person, less than five minutes long, and must involve the use of your artifact. Work to draw the audience into your scene and interest them in your tale from another land!

Role-Play

Brainstorm
Use the questions below to help you think about the scene you will present to the class.

1. Who are the main characters in this scene?
   _____

2. Where does the scene take place?
   _____

3. What objects do the characters use in the scene?
   _____

4. What problem is the focus of the scene?
   _____

5. How is the problem resolved?
   _____

Before You Turn It In
1. Does your descriptive paragraph clearly relate the artifact to the character who uses it?
2. Is your presentation written in the voice of the character and does it make use of the chosen artifact?

Project Designer's Tag

Role-Play Project
Name _____
Title of Book _____
Author _____
Genre _____
Date _____

Mystery Marionette

Teacher Guide

Skills Covered
- identifying character traits
- using the writing process

Project Description

Students use their creativity to design and create flat, paper marionettes with three-dimensional details. These puppets illustrate student interpretations of main characters from selected books. Each student also composes a five-clue riddle to introduce his/her character to others. Each clue should give a little more specific information than the preceding one.

Material Suggestions

Keeping material ideas and construction tips broad will allow for the greatest variety of finished marionettes. Involve the class in brainstorming a list of possibilities for creating and clothing their puppets. Your list may include recyclable materials such as fabric, wallpaper scraps, clay, stiff strips of corrugated cardboard, and narrow pieces of wood or sticks. String, yarn, jute, or some similar material is needed to suspend the puppet.

Tips to Introduce

Bring in examples of marionette puppets or share pictures of them. As a class, discuss the qualities that make a marionette different from other types of puppets. This way, you can generate the key expectations before introducing the take-home project.

Classroom Connections

The riddle is a great language arts topic. Find a book of riddles and read samples to the class. As you read and students try to answer, encourage them to notice how closely linked riddles are to puns; many of them depend on a play on words for their solutions.

Display and Presentation

Each student will share both the marionette and the riddle with the class. Classmates will have the opportunity to try to guess the marionette's identity based on the riddle clues provided.

Mystery Marionette

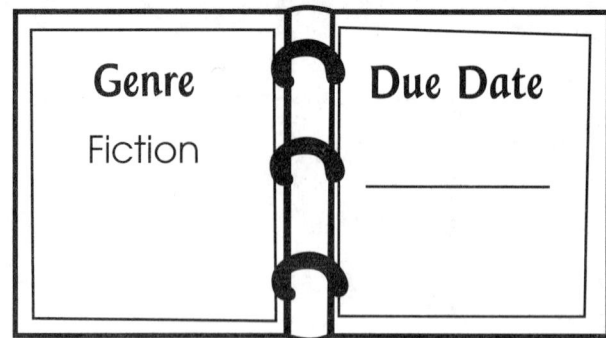

Use your creativity to design a flat, jointed marionette with three-dimensional details. This marionette should show the way you picture a main character in your chosen book. You will also complete a "Who Am I?" riddle with five clues to introduce your classmates to your character in a clever way.

Material Suggestions

You will be constructing your marionette's body from heavy paper, cardboard, or poster board. Brad clips will allow movable joints. You will need to use sticks or dowels and string or yarn to operate your marionette. Choose a variety of other materials to decorate and dress your puppet.

Project Requirements

1. Select a novel or other work of fiction and have it approved. Read your book, and choose your favorite character from the story. Use the web on page 38 to help you record character traits as you read.

2. Design and create your marionette. Start by designing a head, body, arms, and legs to cut out of your poster board. Decide how you will make movable arms and legs, and how you will attach them to string.

3. Make a crossed-stick control from sticks or dowels.

4. Before you attach your puppet to the strings and controls, make three-dimensional features for it—hair from yarn, a nose from clay, eyes from beads—these are just a few ideas. You will also need to decide how to clothe your puppet.

5. Create a "Who Am I?" riddle that is five sentences long. Each of your five clues should give a little more information than the one before.

Mystery Marionette

6. Read your riddle draft carefully. Make sure none of your clues make the answer too obvious. Revise, edit, and rewrite or type the riddle. The completed riddle should be mounted to a piece of poster board that measures 10" x 12" so it can be displayed near your marionette.

7. Include your name on the bottom right-hand corner of your riddle. Then write the name of your character on the back of the board so people can flip the poster board to see who the mystery marionette is. Complete the Project Designer's Tag and tape or glue it to the back of the board, also.

Here is your schedule for the Mystery Marionette project:

☐ Week 1—Select book. Get approval. Read.

☐ Week 2—Select character. Design basic puppet.

☐ Week 3—Add three-dimensional features to marionette. Dress and decorate. Rig to strings.

☐ Week 4—Compose five-part riddle. Edit and mount final copy on poster board.

Check When Done

Presentation Guidelines

You will present your finished marionette to the class and then read the riddle clues to see if anyone can guess the character. Practice reading your clues aloud, pausing after each clue to give the audience a chance to guess the character.

It can be very challenging to get a marionette to move the way you want it to, so be sure to practice. For an added challenge, you might want to pick a favorite part of the text and say the lines while creating movements with your marionette.

Mystery Marionette

Brainstorm

Use the web below to help you record character traits as you read.

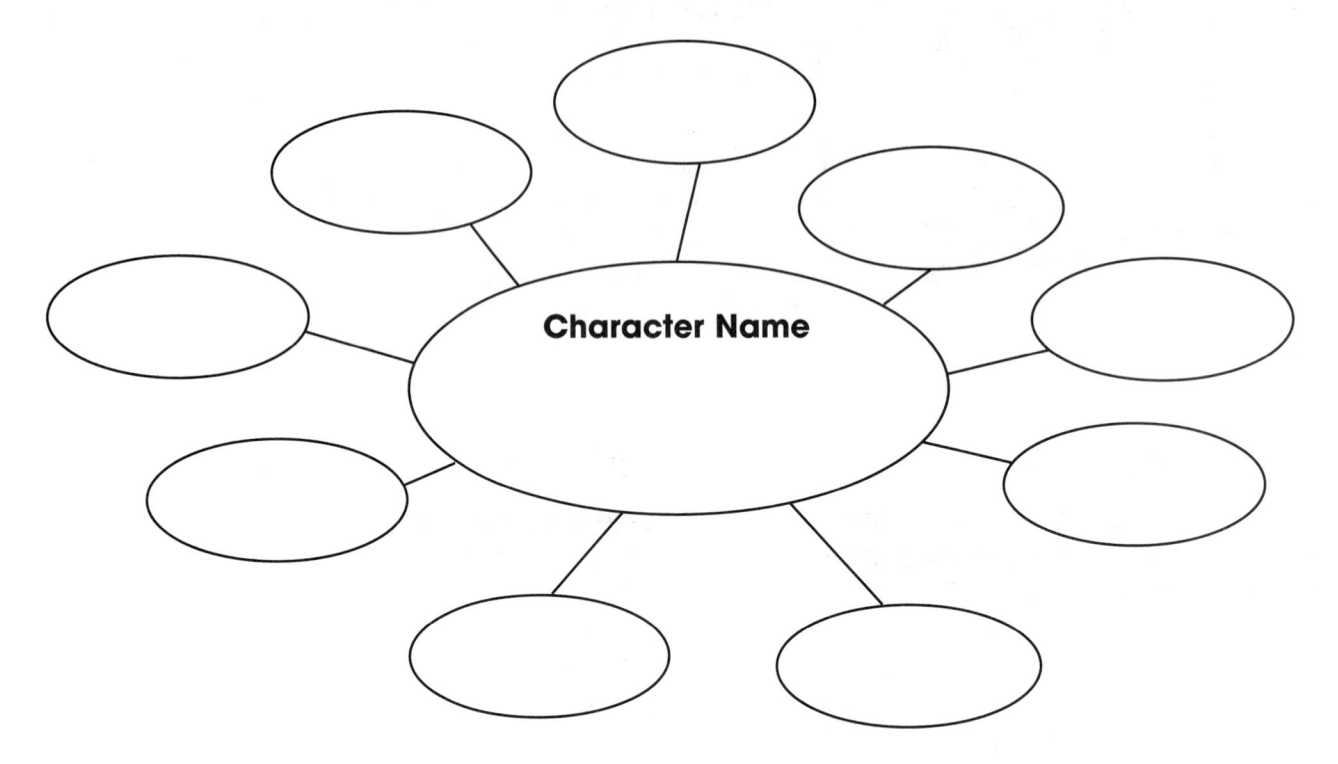

(Character web with "Character Name" in center and 8 surrounding blank ovals)

Before You Turn It In

1. Does marionette's construction show creative use of craft and/or recycled materials?
2. Do riddle clues progress without giving away marionette's identity?

Project Designer's Tag

Mystery Marionette Project

Name _____

Title of Book _____

Author _____

Genre _____

Date _____

Quality Character Banner

Teacher Guide

Skills Covered
- reading poetry
- identifying character traits
- compare and contrast

Project Description
Students create banners that are decorated on both sides to display "quality characteristics" of characters from ballad or story-telling poems. Students compare and contrast the chosen character trait to the same or similar trait of their own.

Material Suggestions
You may decide to provide poster board or large sheets of construction paper plus yarn, string, or twine; or you may set size requirements for the banners and ask students to supply their own materials.

Tips to Introduce
Prior to sending this project home, take time in class to sharpen your students' skill for noting the qualities of characters in poems you read aloud during class. Discuss why the author of a given poem might have decided to select certain qualities for the main character. How do those qualities affect the events laid out in the poem? You might choose to have small groups of students work cooperatively to create descriptive posters, each defining and illustrating qualities featured in this project.

Classroom Connections
Select some ballads or story-telling poems for your class to compare and contrast. Choose a hero (Paul Revere), a hero-criminal (Robin Hood or the Highwayman), or a villain (the Pied Piper). See if your students know any of these stories before you begin reading the poems. Ask them to determine the primary character trait of each person featured in the poems.

Display and Presentation
The finished banners can hang in the classroom, hallway, school lobby, library/media center, or even in the main office or lunchroom. You might even contact your local library to see if they would like to display your banners to celebrate reading month or poetry day.

Quality Character Banner

Genre: Ballad or story-telling poem

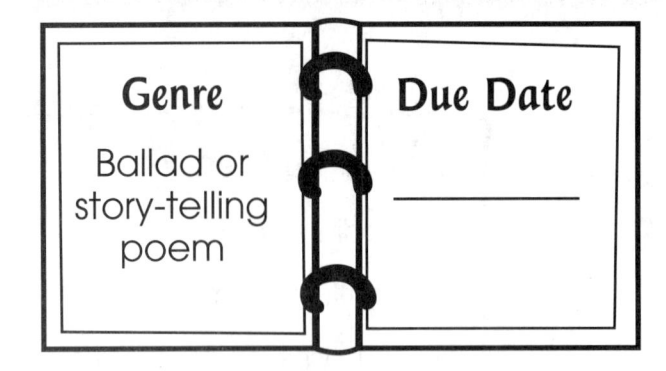

Due Date: _____

While reading a poem of your choice, you will pick one "quality" characteristic of the main character and compare and contrast it with a strength of your own. Then, you will create a two-sided banner to display your work.

Material Suggestions

Your 12" x 18" banner should be made on sturdy paper or poster board. Use string, yarn, or twine to create a hanger for the banner. The writing on the banner will involve the use of markers, paints, crayons, or another medium. You may want to make streamers from ribbons or strips of wrapping paper.

Project Requirements

1. Read several ballads and story poems. Select one and have it approved.
2. Decide the shape and design of your banner. Be sure it is large enough to display the following:

    Side 1: Title of poem, author's name, and paragraph persuading others to read the poem.

    Side 2: Headline of quality characteristic, one paragraph describing how the character in the poem displayed the trait, and second paragraph describing how you have displayed the same trait. Use the table on page 42 to record your notes before writing.

3. Choose one of the quality characteristics below as a trait displayed by the character in your poem. The trait you pick will be the headline for side 2 of your banner.

    a. Problem-solving—seeking solutions in times of trouble.
    b. Responsibility—being accountable for your actions.
    c. Perseverance—continuing on despite problems.

Quality Character Banner

    d. Initiative—taking the lead and doing something because it needs to be done.

    e. Flexibility—being able to make changes when needed.

    f. Courage—being brave and positive even when difficulties are overwhelming.

4. Draft your paragraphs as described in step 2. Ask an adult to offer suggestions for improvement. Edit your paragraphs.

5. Make your banner. Copy your headlines and paragraphs onto it, using your best writing. Then color and decorate.

6. Punch two holes in both upper corners of your banner. Thread yarn, string, or twine to act as a hanger.

7. Complete and cut out the Project Designer's Tag and bring it in with your banner.

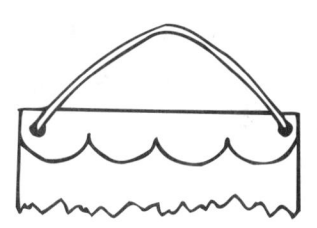

Here is your schedule for the Quality Character Banner project:

☐   Week 1—Select poem and have it approved. Sketch shape for banner.

☐   Week 2—Select characteristic of poem character and self. Draft paragraphs. Edit.

☐   Week 3—Cut out and letter banner. Decorate and finish.

Check When Done

Presentation Guidelines

Your banner will hang on display for others to read and admire. Make sure your banner looks great on both sides, is colorful, and is easy to read!

© Carson-Dellosa   0-7424-2735-8 *Book Projects to Send Home*

Quality Character Banner

Brainstorm

Use the chart below to record times when you and the main character both displayed a quality character trait.

	Character	Me
Trait		
Times When Trait Was Displayed		

Before You Turn It In

1. Does your banner show a positive quality of poem character and yourself?
2. Are your paragraphs motivating and convincing?

Project Designer's Tag

Quality Character Banner Project
Name _____
Title of Book _____
Author _____
Genre _____
Date _____

Far-Out Travel Brochure

Teacher Guide

Skills Covered
- reading science fiction or fantasy
- identifying setting
- persuasive writing

Project Description
As a travel agent for the See the World Travel Agency, each student creates a travel brochure featuring the setting of a fantasy or science fiction book. Students will present their brochures in TV-commercial form, speaking about setting as a must-see vacation spot.

Material Suggestions
Students need 8 1/2" x 11" sheets of paper, markers, paints, and other media to complete brochures.

Tips to Introduce
Invite a travel agent to your class or gather a collection of travel brochures from exotic locations. Form small groups and have each answer the questions below after looking at a travel brochure.

- What is the most eye-catching part of the brochure?
- What words or phrases are memorable?
- How do the pictures help sell the travel location?
- What facts are included on the brochure about the location and about the costs of visiting there?

Classroom Connections
Have students design "the perfect vacation spot." Have students design the vacation setting with only themselves in mind. What would the place be like if the student could have his or her own way in every detail? Students will delight in this project, and it will help them brainstorm for the types of details they should include in their brochures and in the TV commercials, too.

Display and Presentation
Display completed brochures on bulletin boards, as bookcase toppers, or as a tabletop reading display in the library/media center. A hand-held microphone or a cardboard-box "television" can add pizzazz to the presentations.

Far-Out Travel Brochure

Genre: Science Fiction or Fantasy

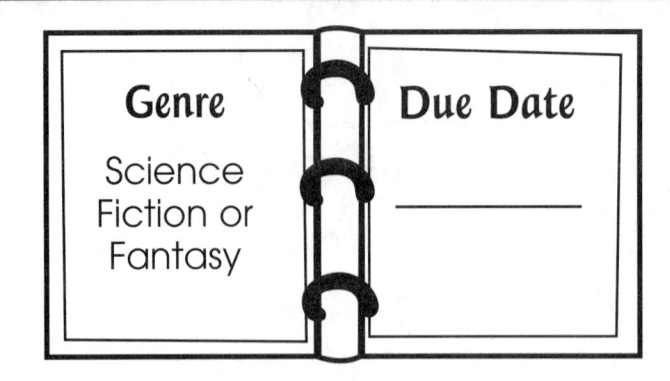

Due Date: _____

You have just been hired as a travel agent for the See the World Travel Agency! Your first assignment is to design and produce a travel brochure based on the science fiction or fantasy book you've read. The text and illustrations should entice your reader to visit the far-out location featured in your brochure.

Material Suggestions

A sheet of $8\frac{1}{2}$" x 11" paper, folded in half; crayons, markers, or paint pens; other media (such as stickers) as desired.

Project Requirements

1. Select a science fiction or fantasy book. Have it approved. Begin reading.
2. As you read the book, determine the setting that will be featured as the focus of your brochure.
3. The form on page 46 will help you brainstorm ideas for your writing. The brochure must include the following:
   a. An interesting cover, with an illustration of the story setting. The name of the location must be easy to read. Also include "This brochure was prepared by (your name)."
   b. A list of creatures in this fantasy location (main characters). Provide illustrations of the "friendly inhabitants."
   c. A detailed description of the location, telling why it would be an ideal vacation spot.
   d. Create a description and illustration of the "mayor" of this location (the author of the book).
   e. Design a map of the setting with fantasy directions to reach this destination.
4. Use lots of color and creative lettering to make your brochure eye-catching and fun!

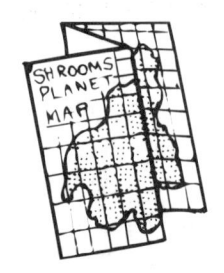

Far-Out Travel Brochure

5. Once your brochure is completed, start making notes about the best-selling points of your imaginary vacation spot. You will be creating a TV commercial of one to three minutes, selling your book setting to prospective travelers.

6. Write a script for your commercial, and rehearse it in front of family members. Make sure you have a lead-in that grabs audience attention. Be concise, using only the most interesting details. Work hard to convince your audience that your setting is a great vacation destination.

7. Complete and cut out the Project Designer's Tag. Attach it to the brochure.

Here is your schedule for the Far-Out Travel Brochure project:

- ☐ Week 1—Choose your book. Get it approved. Begin reading.
- ☐ Week 2—Take notes while reading about the book's setting. Write text and draw a plan for your brochure.
- ☐ Week 3—Edit your brochure text. Finish brochure.
- ☐ Week 4—Write, edit, and rehearse TV commercial.

Check When Done

Presentation Guidelines

You will be your convincing best as we listen to your TV commercial in class. Your brochure will be on display for all to enjoy.

Far-Out Travel Brochure

Brainstorm
Fill in the form below with details from the book you read to help you think about what to write on your travel brochure.

Location name: _____

How to get there: _____

What you'll see there: _____

Who lives there: _____

What they look like: _____

Mayor of this location: _____

Best reasons to visit this location: _____

Before You Turn It In
1. Are both your brochure and your commercial persuasive?
2. Do the contents of the brochure correlate to the setting and details of the book you read?

Project Designer's Tag

Far-Out Travel Brochure Project
Name _____
Title of Book _____
Author _____
Genre _____
Date _____

Student Self-Evaluation Form

Name _____ Date _____

Project Title _____

Check the box that shows how you think you did.

Criteria	Excellent	Good	Fair	Needs Improvement
Project shows personal best.				
Written work is well organized, neat, and accurate.				
Project design shows thoughtful planning.				
Project completely meets requirements.				

My favorite part of the project was _____

_____.

My least favorite part of the project was _____

_____.

Suggested Titles for Fifth-Grade Readers

A Single Shard—by Linda Sue Park

A Year Down Yonder—by Richard Peck

Anastasia Krupnik—by Lois Lowry

And Then What Happened, Paul Revere?—by Jean Fritz

Bud, Not Buddy—by Christopher Paul Curtis

Crispin: The Cross of Lead—by Avi

Frindle—by Andrew Clements

Hatchet—by Gary Paulsen

Holes—by Louis Sachar

I, Too, Sing America: Three Centuries of African American Poetry—by Catherine Clinton

Johnny Tremain—by Esther Forbes

Love That Dog—by Sharon Creech

Miracle's Boys—by Jacqueline Woodson

Nothing's Fair in the Fifth Grade—by Barthe DeClements

Out of the Dust—by Karen Hesse

Phineas Gage: A Gruesome But True Story About Brain Science—by John Fleischman

Rocket Boys: A Memoir—by Homer H. Hickman

Roll of Thunder, Hear My Cry—by Mildred D. Taylor

Slam!—by Walter Dean Myers

Sticks—by Joan Bauer

The Book of Three—by Lloyd Alexander

The Clay Marble—by Ho

The Dark Is Rising—by Susan Cooper

The Midwife's Apprentice—by Karen Cushman

The View from Saturday—by E. L. Konigsburg

Walk Two Moons—by Sharon Creech

When the Tripods Came—by John Christopher